PAST AND PRESENT
CENSORSHIP
PHILIP STEELE

Protest against restrictions on free speech in the United States.

HEINEMANN

First published by Heinemann Children's Reference, 1992, a division of Heinemann Educational Books Ltd., Halley Court, Jordan Hill, Oxford OX2 8EJ.

OXFORD LONDON EDINBURGII
MADRID PARIS ATHENS BOLOGNA
MELBOURNE SYDNEY AUCKLAND SINGAPORE
TOKYO IBADAN NAIROBI GABORONE HARARE
PORTSMOUTH NH (USA)

Devised and produced by Zoe Books Limited
15 Worthy Lane, Winchester, SO23 7AB, England

Edited by Charlotte Rolfe
Picture research by Faith Perkins
Designed by Julian Holland

Printed in Hong Kong

A CIP catalogue record for this book is available from the British Library.

ISBN 0 431 00668 7

Photographic acknowledgements

The author and publishers wish to acknowledge, with thanks, the following photographic sources: Camera Press pp 35; 36: Hulton Deutsch Collection pp10; 13: Magnum pp 6 (photograph Marc Riboud); 26 (photograph Fred Mayer); 39 (photograph Erich Hartmann): Rex features pp 24; 29; 31: Topham Picture Library pp title page; 4; 8; 17; 22; 27; 42

The cover photograph is courtesy of Magnum/Ian Berry

The publishers have made every effort to trace the copyright holders, but if they have inadvertently overlooked any, they will be pleased to make the necessary arrangement at the first opportunity.

CONTENTS

WHAT IS CENSORSHIP?

Keeping out the press. An American news photographer is directed away from an Israeli-occupied town on the West Bank. The Israeli army had just broken up a Palestinian protest march and declared the town a no-go area for reporters.

CONTROL THROUGH CENSORSHIP

Censorship often makes headline news. Scarcely a week passes without some newspaper announcing events such as: 'POP RECORD TAKEN OFF AIR', 'CALL FOR BAN ON TV VIOLENCE', or 'NEW PLAY ORDERED TO CLOSE'. The headlines may also refer to important issues of the day, for example 'GOVERNMENT SETS UP PRESS WATCHDOG COMMITTEE'. During a particular crisis, such as a major strike, a natural disaster, or a war, the press might ask the question 'ARE WE BEING TOLD THE WHOLE TRUTH?' The stories which follow such headlines may be for, or against, a particular form of censorship.

Censorship does not only concern people in the communications **media** such as broadcasting, publishing and the arts. It concerns every one of us, because it affects our basic rights and freedom as individuals. When we turn on the television, or open a book or newspaper, the information we see and read has been selected by somebody else. We may ask ourselves, is this the truth – are we getting the whole story? Some people believe that there should be controls on what we see, read or hear, because there are things which cause offence. Do people need to be protected?

Our answers to these questions depend on our own opinions and beliefs. People will always argue, first about what counts as censorship, and second, whether censorship is right, wrong, or simply unavoidable in a particular situation.

> 'The liberty of the individual must be thus far limited; he must not make himself a nuisance to other people.'
>
> *John Stuart Mill,*
> *English philosopher (1806-1873)*

Censorship is in the news, but it is also a part of the news-making process itself. Censorship is the **vetting**,

A Soviet soldier places his hand in front of the camera lens. In most countries, photographing members of the armed forces or the police is discouraged or forbidden, especially in times of crisis.

or official examination, of material that is written, painted, published, filmed or broadcast. It may take place before the material is made public, or afterwards.

Anything 'unsuitable' may then be removed or **suppressed**. Sometimes, whole books, plays, exhibitions or programmes may be banned. Discussing or reporting certain items may be forbidden. Particular individuals or organizations may be refused permission to speak in public. In all its forms, censorship controls what people see or read, and therefore what they think.

The word 'censorship' often refers to more than the vetting of a particular news report or piece of writing. Sometimes it is used to describe a policy of secrecy, or suppression of public information. All governments have **official secrets**, or information which the public is not allowed to know. Governments often claim that some information must be restricted in this way in order to protect the country and the existing freedom of its citizens. Some people may disagree; they may question the way in which a government defines the word 'freedom'.

Most people agree that absolute or total freedom is not possible. Each person in the community must compromise, giving up individual freedoms in the interest of others. However, many people care passionately about the degree of freedom that is permitted within a society. The extent of censorship carried out in any country shows us whether that country is as free as it claims to be.

CENSORSHIP IN ACTION

Sometimes censorship is obvious to everybody. Newspapers are published with blanks in them where news stories have been officially censored by the government, copies of a particular book are withdrawn from shops, or a television programme is banned. But very often, censorship is difficult to see. Anyone who reports news has to select certain facts and leave out others. However, if they deliberately restrict the kind of information they are passing on to the public, then they are carrying out a form of censorship.

In August 1990, American troops were sent to Saudi Arabia, after Iraq had invaded its neighbour, the Gulf state of Kuwait. The following five months led to the Gulf War with Iraq. In the United States there were nightly broadcasts about the Gulf situation. There were also major public protests against the war in several big American cities. However, only about one percent of national news coverage at this time even referred to these protests. A group called FAIR (Fairness and Accuracy in Reporting) claimed that this was not enough. They also noted that no foreign policy experts who had links with the anti-war movement appeared on the nightly news during this period.

Was this censorship? The United States government hadn't directly ordered the big news companies to keep criticism of the war off the air, but they did so, voluntarily. They could argue that such items were of

The front page of a Rhodesian newspaper during the country's struggle for independence as modern Zimbabwe. Inside the small box half-way down the right hand column it explains that all news stories and pictures have been subjected to government censorship. The blank space in this issue of *The Chronicle* (19 November 1965) shows that the main front page story was suppressed by the government censor.

little interest to the public anyway. On the other hand, people were not hearing both sides of a very important question: the involvement of their country in a dangerous and expensive war.

Censorship may also be the result of commercial pressures. A newspaper owner may refuse to print articles if they criticize a company that pays to advertise in his publications. A publisher might remove information from a book if it criticizes a foreign country in which she sells her books. Both might argue that they have the right to publish what they like. The reading public might claim that they have a right to be informed. Arguments about censorship often involve clashes between individual rights and freedoms.

WHO CARRIES OUT CENSORSHIP?

Censorship may be carried out by governments or by local councils. Education departments, for example, can control which textbooks are used in class or which subjects are taught.

When an army is engaged in warfare, officers may practise censorship by cutting sections from letters written home by the troops, or from reports by journalists. They fear that such information might give away secrets to the enemy.

A powerful religious organization may practise its own form of censorship by suppressing material which it believes is unsuitable for people to read. Some works of literature which are very famous today have in the past been banned by the Church.

Other forms of censorship are often used within clubs, political parties, or commercial companies. Sometimes a company or a political party may choose to suppress certain information about themselves and their activities, because they know it will reduce their profits, or their popularity, if made public. Within families, parents may censor what their children read or watch on video or television. Censorship affects us all.

CENSORSHIP IN HISTORY

This painting shows the Italian astronomer Galileo on trial for his scientific ideas at the Pope's court in 1633. His theory of the universe was banned by the Roman Catholic Church, but was smuggled out of Italy to the Protestant countries of northern Europe.

'History would be an excellent thing if only it were true.'

Leo Tolstoy,
Russian writer (1828-1910)

THE EMPEROR WHO BURNED BOOKS

In the ancient civilizations of India and China, it was common practice for rulers to destroy the documents of previous dynasties, or ruling families. The rulers wanted only their own version of events to be passed down to future generations.

The Chinese philosopher Kong Fuzi, or Confucius, who was born in 551BC, opposed this form of censorship. However, Confucius' own writings were amongst the many books later destroyed by the Chinese emperor Qin Shi Huangdi in 213BC. This powerful ruler believed that literature should be strictly practical, and should deal with matters such as farming or medicine. He ordered an encyclopaedia to be written under the strict control of his government. Works that contained critical or **dissident** views were to be burned by his chancellor, Li Si. Scholars who disagreed with him were to be executed. When the emperor himself died, his tomb was guarded by hundreds of statues made of terracotta. Each one represented a soldier of his army. He wished his authority to survive even after he was dead.

THE ROMAN CENSORS

The word 'censor' comes from the Latin language. *Censere* meant 'to decree, to rate, to judge, to assess or to pronounce as an opinion'. From 443BC onwards, two public officials served the state of Rome as 'censors'. They had all kinds of duties. They organized the 'census', or population count, and they awarded public contracts. They also supervised public behaviour and questions of morals. They could punish people and send them into exile for writing **immoral** or **treasonable** books that argued against the accepted way of life, or against the government itself. They often did so. The job was a powerful one, and it was later held by some of the Roman emperors.

One of Rome's most successful poets was Ovid, born at Sulmo in 43BC. He wrote three books under the title *The Art of Love*. When these were condemned as **obscene**, or immoral, by the emperor Augustus in AD8, Ovid was banished to Tomis, a remote town by the Black Sea. Many people said he was sent away for political reasons. Ovid died in exile in AD17.

Many of the great works of ancient Greek and Roman literature were collected together at a great library in the Egyptian city of Alexandria. They were written out on scrolls of papyrus. In their own way, the librarians acted as censors, deciding which works were worth copying. They also changed or left out passages as they thought fit. Several centuries later, the library suffered a more extreme form of censorship. It was burnt and destroyed by Christian and Muslim invaders who felt that many of the writings were **blasphemous**, or insulting to their religious beliefs.

RELIGION AND THE PRINTING PRESSES

The early Christians had often been persecuted in the Roman empire, but by the beginning of the fourteenth century their religion had been formally recognized by the Roman emperor Constantine. As the Christian Church grew in power, however, it too turned to strict, or **authoritarian** control over people's lives.

During the Middle Ages, the Islamic and Jewish scriptures were banned throughout Christian Europe. Earlier Christians had felt it was their duty to read these works, so that they could better understand the arguments of their religious rivals. Now, the new universities held special courts which vetted all written work. People who wrote or made statements which contradicted the views of the Church were declared to be **heretics**. They were often tortured and burnt to death.

A seventeenth century book printer at work in a Dutch town. The invention of the printing press helped to spread people's ideas more widely in books and pamphlets.

When printing reached Europe in the 1440s, the authorities became nervous. Until now literature had been written by hand and kept locked up in monasteries and universities. Now, hundreds of copies could be printed and sold to the general public. In the German town of Mainz, where modern printing began, the archbishop demanded a public censorship office in 1485.

In many European countries, rulers introduced systems of licensing printers. If a printer published books which were not approved, his licence would not be renewed. This method of censorship was used in England until 1695. By then, so much literature was being printed that it became impossible to keep track of each item.

In 1559 Pope Paul IV set up a censorship body, the Congregation of the Index, to vet all books published in Roman Catholic countries. Its rules were tightened up in 1564 by Pope Pius IV, and again in 1571 by Pius V. The Index of Prohibited Books contained works by the Dutch thinker Erasmus, and by well-known Protestant Christians such as Martin Luther and John Calvin.

Books which were thought to be immoral, such as those by the French writer François Rabelais (c.1491-1553), were also banned by the Index. Paintings were censored for the same reason, and in Rome, nine figures portrayed by the great artist Michelangelo (1475-1564) were painted over.

THE CRY FOR FREEDOM

In the eighteenth century the power of the Church and of Europe's kings and queens was challenged by many people. Books and pamphlets demanding liberty and human rights were banned or heavily censored by the authorities. However, they were often circulated illegally and reached a wide audience. In 1762 Jean-Jacques Rousseau's *Le Contrat Social* ('The Social Contract') was published in the Netherlands in order to avoid a ban in France. Its opening words read: 'Man is born free and everywhere he is in chains'.

In 1776 Britain's North American colonies declared their independence, with a call for liberty and an end to strict authoritarian rule by very few people. Such views were unacceptable in Europe. In 1782 a revolutionary play called *Die Räuber* ('The Robbers') was banned in the German state of Württemberg. Its author, Friedrich von Schiller, was arrested. However,

Europe's rulers were sitting on a powder keg. In 1789 the French king and his government were overthrown by a violent revolution of ordinary people who wanted a better life and a more equal say in the government of their country. The new French Assembly could now triumphantly announce that 'free communication of thoughts is one of the most precious rights of man.'

The English political writer Thomas Paine took part in the American and French revolutions. His straightforward style was popular among many readers, and he used it to call for an end to rule by kings and queens – as he put it 'to inherit a government is to inherit a people, as if they were flocks and herds.' He explained his views in *The Rights of Man* which was published in England in 1792. The book was an enormous success, and sold 200 000 copies in less than a year. The government accused Paine of blasphemy, because he questioned the god-given right of royalty to inherit and rule a country. It also accused him of treason towards his country. Paine escaped to France at the beginning of the trial, but a number of others who had been involved in printing and publishing his work were fined or sent to prison.

Thomas Paine was not the only writer to be politically censored at this time. A number of newspapers were prosecuted for printing articles and letters which criticized the English government, or showed sympathy for the ideas of the French revolution. In the meantime, new ideas about democracy were gaining ground elsewhere. In America in 1791, a 'Bill of Rights' was included in the new constitution, which guaranteed free speech to all citizens, a principle close to the heart of Thomas Paine.

THE FEAR OF REVOLUTION

Events in France had terrified kings, queens and government leaders across Europe. The revolution had produced its own 'Reign of Terror', during which the French king, Louis XVI, was executed, and thousands of others were killed or terrified into silence. However, this did not stop the flow of new political ideas which were now gaining popular support in many countries. As the nineteenth century advanced, many people began to demand change. Events in France and America had at least proved that this was possible.

In countries such as Russia, then under the authoritarian rule of the royal tsars, strict censorship was used to prevent the spread of these revolutionary ideas. The tsars had their own secret police force, and anyone caught criticizing the tsar or his rule, was sent into exile in the wastelands of Siberia.

PRIVATE CENSORSHIP

As more and more people were able to read, censorship went beyond politics. It was not only carried out by governments and courts of law. There were many groups and individuals who saw themselves as protectors of public morals. They took it upon themselves to decide what was suitable reading for women and children in the home, for example. Books and paintings had to suit the often **prudish** tastes of the new middle classes. Thomas Bowdler (1754-1825) produced *The Family Shakespeare*, in which whole sections of the great poet's text were cut out, in case they offended people. The word 'bowdlerize' is still used today. It means to **expurgate**, or remove any sections of a work which are considered immoral.

However, there were some plays which Bowdler found he could not expurgate without reducing the story to nonsense. Shakespeare's *Othello* was one such example. Bowdler's advice on this great play was simple: 'The subject is little suited to family reading... I would advise transferring it from the parlour to the cabinet.' In other words, it should be placed safely under lock and key!

FREEDOM OR CONTROL ?

Independent newspapers may be free from the control of the press barons, but they may also come under other pressures. Here, the editor holds the two final editions of the *Transvaal Post*, a newspaper banned in 1980 for criticizing the South African government and its policies.

In 1916 the Irish writer James Joyce wrote a book called *A Portrait of the Artist as a Young Man*. In it, the hero, named Stephen Dedalus, states defiantly: 'I will not serve that in which I no longer believe, whether it call itself my home, my fatherland or my church: and I will try to express myself in some mode of life or art as freely as I can...'

Many of the artists of the early twentieth century wished to see how far they could push the boundaries of free expression. Their aim was to shock the public into looking at life anew. In paintings, the human form was broken up into geometric shapes. Newspapers were cut up and pasted into patterns. Different photographs were joined together to make pictures, and artists portrayed a world of disturbing dreams. A toilet seat was even exhibited as a work of art!

Bands played jazz, the music of Black America, which seemed to break all the traditional rules of European composition. Writers jumbled up words and wrote down their innermost thoughts as they spilled out on to the page. They wrote of love affairs in a frank and realistic way which would have been unheard of in the previous century.

The public was often confused. The authorities were outraged and took action in the courts of law. Art exhibitions were closed and shows were raided by the police. Books were banned, including works by James Joyce and the writer D.H. Lawrence (1885-1930). This extract from the *Daily Mirror* newspaper in London (6.7.1929) describes one such incident: 'A volume of poems by D.H. Lawrence, which was seized by the Post Office while being sent from Italy, where Mr Lawrence is at present living, was later released and has just been published. His latest prose work, *Lady Chatterley's Lover*, was privately printed in Florence, but its publication in this country was banned.'

NEW WAYS OF COMMUNICATING

The worlds of art, music, literature and politics were now reaching a far wider audience, thanks to new technology. Photography, record players (or 'phonographs') and cinema had all been developed in the nineteenth century. Speech was first transmitted by radio in 1906, and regular broadcasts were first made in the United States in 1921, by KDKA in Pittsburgh. Television was first demonstrated in 1925 and by the second half of the century most families in western countries had a television at home.

The press also changed enormously during the twentieth century. New printing methods made it possible to produce glossy colour magazines for the first time. In western countries powerful people, nicknamed press barons, owned large numbers of newspapers and magazines. By the 1960s and 1970s huge companies had developed which controlled not just newspapers and magazines, but printing and broadcasting interests around the world.

NEW CONTROLS

In Britain, radio, and later, television broadcasts were the responsibility of a public corporation founded in 1927, the British Broadcasting Corporation (BBC). Broadcasting was funded by licence fees. The BBC was intended to be independent from both state and commercial control – advertisements were not broadcast in Britain until 1955. In the United States, commercial interests were in control from the start, but broadcasting was supervised by government bodies such as the Federal Communications Commission of 1934.

Cinemas posed new problems. In both Europe and America the new medium of film was widely criticized by the authorities and yet it was hugely popular. The film industry was asked to control its own standards. At the same time state and local bodies were set up which vetted the suitability of films for children as well as adults. Institutions such as the British Board of Film Censors had sweeping powers. Many films were banned or cut, and no film could be shown in public without the Board's approval.

> 'The efficiency of the truly national leader consists mainly of preventing the people's attention from becoming divided, and of always concentrating it on a single enemy.'
>
> *Adolf Hitler, 'Mein Kampf', 1924*

CENSORSHIP IN A POLICE STATE

Some governments of the twentieth century were quick to use the new technology for their own purposes. In 1933, the Nazi party seized control of the German government under their leader Adolf Hitler. The Nazis immediately started their campaign to stifle free speech and impose their own idea of a superior German race. It affected every aspect of public and private life. In an effort to make the cultural world speak with one voice (their own), they banned the works of hundreds of writers, artists, film makers and musicians. Many were forced to flee from Germany. Those who remained were silenced by fear, imprisonment or even execution.

Religious, cultural and leisure organizations were closed down or taken over by the Nazis in order to increase their power. Special feature films shown in the cinemas promoted the Hitler Youth organization, and encouraged extreme nationalist and **racist** views in young audiences. The new artistic freedoms that had appeared at the beginning of the twentieth century were savagely suppressed; books were burned in special ceremonies in towns all over Germany.

COMMUNISTS AND THE MEDIA

The Soviet Union had been formed after a communist revolution in Russia in 1917. Censorship was a basic part of the new state. It was claimed that the communications media were a weapon in the fight for social justice, and that only the Communist party was able to carry out that fight. The founder of the Soviet Union, Vladimir Ilyich Lenin, put it simply: 'The truth is partisan' – meaning that it takes sides.

The Soviets scorned the western view of the media. The western press was not free, they said, because it was controlled by the rich and powerful in order to promote their own interests. The Soviets believed that the western press was becoming the slave of the factory owners and the advertising industry, who paid large sums for advertising space in newspapers and periodicals.

Under the leadership of Joseph Stalin (1879-1953), however, it looked as if the Soviet press had become the slave of a dictator. No journalist could stand up to his secret police, his threats of imprisonment or execution. People who had fallen from favour were removed from official photographs and taken out of the history books. It was as if they had never existed. Foreign broadcasts were drowned out by a process called **jamming**.

Much later, under the leadership of Mikhail Gorbachev, in the 1980s, a programme of reform, or *glasnost*, was successfully introduced in the Soviet Union. Admittedly, censorship remained. However, opposition groups now had a voice and foreign broadcasts were no longer jammed. In 1991, a new television channel was started, to provide an opportunity for free debate and criticism of government policies.

WAR AND PEACE

The twentieth century was marked by some of the most horrific wars ever known. Conflict reached every part of the world. In both the First World War (1914-18) and the Second World War (1939-45) censorship went far beyond keeping military communications secret. In Britain, newspapers which might have criticized the war effort were closed down and important truths were concealed in the press and in radio broadcasts. Even the general public was encouraged to be secretive, with slogans such as 'Careless talk costs lives'.

Fewer people were aware that censorship continued in peacetime, or recognized it. In 1953 the

In the 1950s Senator Joseph McCarthy (left) led a dramatic campaign accusing many American citizens of communist sympathies.

International Press Institute surveyed newspaper editors in over 40 countries. Most agreed that there was a 'growing tendency, in **democratic** as well as in non-democratic countries, to restrict the free gathering of legitimate news'. Many blamed the wartime experience for increased secrecy and censorship. People had become used to hearing the 'official' version of the news.

During the 1950s a 'cold war' existed between the United States and its allies, and the Soviet Union. There was deep dislike and mistrust on both sides, though this never broke out into open warfare. In the United States, a politician called Joseph McCarthy fanned American fears of communism by waging a personal war against any Americans who were suspected communists, or were sympathetic to the ideals of communism or socialism. Many innocent people were brought before powerful government committees to be investigated and accused of 'un-American' activities in front of the television cameras. Actors, film stars and writers under suspicion were encouraged to inform against each other. If they refused, they would not be given any future work by the powerful producers and film companies.

WAR ON TELEVISION

The first major war of the television age occurred between 1964 and 1973, when the United States was fighting to keep communism out of Vietnam. Never before had the horror of warfare been seen night after night on news broadcasts in the home. When a large anti-war protest built up in the United States, many people believed it was the result of the television coverage.

Both British and United States governments learned from this lesson in later conflicts. In 1982 Britain fought Argentina in the Malvinas, or Falkland Islands. News of the conflict was strictly controlled. The British Ministry of Defence issued misleading information and censored reports without indicating that they had done so. Reports from the battle areas were sometimes delayed or lost. The British government clashed with the BBC for allowing dissident views to be broadcast, accusing them of disloyalty.

'The first casualty when war comes is truth.'

Hiram Johnson, American senator, 1917

SECRECY AND POLITICS

The women here are demonstrating on behalf of their missing relatives in Argentina. Under the country's military government (1976-82) no opposition was allowed. Over 30 000 people were arrested or simply disappeared. Enquiries were met with silence or further punishment.

STATE SECRETS

Official secrets are items of government information which by law cannot be communicated to the public. In the United States, official government records cannot be published until 25 years after an event has taken place. In Britain the period is now 30 years, or even 100 years for certain items. In 1957, the British government reported a minor fire at a nuclear power station. Not until 1988 was it revealed that this had been a major disaster on a world scale.

> 'Secrecy is the first essential in affairs of state.'
>
> *Duc de Richelieu,*
> *French cardinal and politician (1585-1642)*

In most countries, people who work for the government are forbidden to reveal information about national security, such as military plans or details of relations with other countries. People often argue about the definition of 'national security'. It may include information about trade or industry, or even routine planning decisions by the civil service.

People who release secret or **classified** information to a foreign power may be arrested and tried as spies. Sometimes government employees reveal state secrets to the press because they believe people should know about particular decisions or actions being taken. These so-called **whistle-blowers** may also lose their jobs and be taken to court.

In 1986 a British secret agent named Peter Wright hit the headlines. He had retired to Australia where he wished to publish a book called *Spycatcher*. The book claimed that British agents had actively plotted against the government in the 1970s when Harold Wilson had been prime minister. The Conservative government took Peter Wright to court. It said that when he joined the British secret service, Wright had agreed to obey the Official Secrets Act. He was therefore not entitled to publish his book, even though the accusations contained in the book had already been made in public. Newspapers were even banned from summarizing the book's contents. However, British government lawyers failed to get the book banned in Australia, and soon the British public was reading editions of the book published abroad.

Few people would suggest that a state should reveal secrets which would aid an enemy or put its own citizens at risk. However, many people do argue that governments are unnecessarily secretive and use the laws of secrecy to cover up political scandals and embarrassments.

Villagers look on helplessly as scientists check the soil for radioactivity at a village near Chernobyl, four years after the nuclear accident there in 1986. Details of the accident were made public in a way that had not happened before in the Soviet Union, but local people were still not given full information.

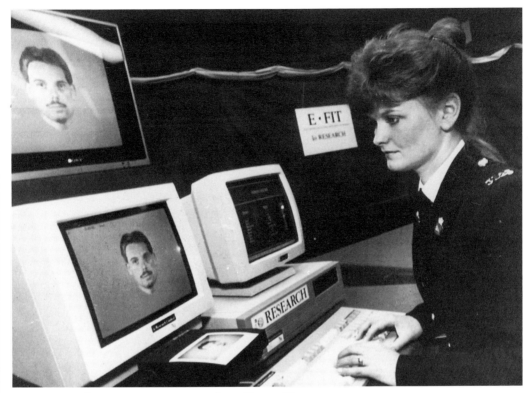

Computer secrets. A police officer uses a computer to build up a picture image of a wanted person.

OPEN FILES?

A Freedom of Information Act was passed in the United States in 1966 and in Australia in 1982. Such laws are limited because they exist alongside official secrets acts, but at least they provide the individual citizen with one way of finding out about some government activities. It is sometimes possible for British or Canadian journalists visiting the United States to find out information that would be classified as secret in their home country.

Such laws are increasingly important in the computer age. The amount of data which can be kept on file is now enormous. Records may be kept on all aspects of someone's life. Detailed information can be kept concerning someone's health, political activities, criminal records, financial status or tax records, work experience, or family details. In Sweden, individuals have the right to check files which concern them, except if these refer to criminal court cases or to well-defined official secrets. Swedes also have the right to see letters sent and received by public officials. In many other countries people are not able to find out what information is being kept on them.

DEALING WITH TERRORISM

In the 1980s the British government chose censorship as a way of dealing with the extreme forces at work in Northern Ireland. In 1988 television and radio interviews were forbidden with members of organizations such as the Provisional wing of the Irish Republican Army (IRA) and the Ulster Defence Association (UDA). Both these groups were committing acts of violence in Northern Ireland. Banning orders were also issued against interviews with Sinn Fein. This political party supported the IRA, and it had a number of elected council representatives and a national member of parliament. However, programmes could be shown in which an actor spoke the words of the person interviewed. In Spain, too, strict censorship laws were passed in the 1980s in order to stifle any publicity for Basques who were fighting the government.

Political censorship against terrorist groups is certainly a double-edged weapon. One problem is that few people can agree how to define the word 'terrorist'. People who some governments call 'terrorist', may be known as 'freedom fighters' by those who support their aims. Some governments use terrorist methods themselves but censor the opposition on the grounds that it is made up of 'terrorists'.

FOREIGN RELATIONS

One important aspect of free speech is the right to communicate across national boundaries. Thomas Paine was happy to campaign in England, France or America. Today he might well run into problems in all

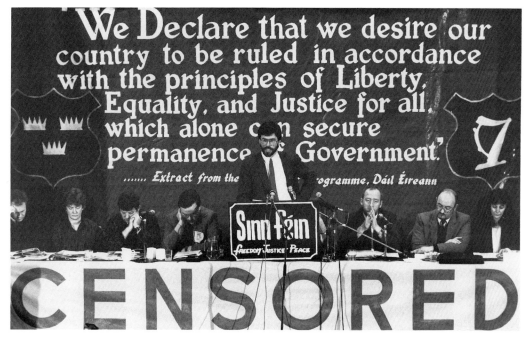

'We Declare that we desire our country to be ruled in accordance with the principles of Liberty, Equality, and Justice for all, which alone can secure permanence of Government.'

.... Extract from the ....ogramme, Dáil Éireann

Sınn Féın
Freedom · Justice · Peace

CENSORED

A Sinn Fein party conference makes its own point about being silenced in the British media.

those countries. France has banned foreign publications which criticize governments friendly to France. The United States regularly refuses entry to well-known foreign writers and journalists with whose political views it disagrees.

It is fairly easy to control the import and export of books or magazines, but satellite television makes a nonsense of national frontiers. In the southern Chinese province of Guangdong many people can receive television from Hong Kong, and so hear opinions which would be censored in their home broadcasts.

POLITICS IN THE MEDIA

It is not just governments that carry out political censorship. Newspapers very often reflect only the political views and interests of their owners. There may be nothing wrong with that in itself. The trouble occurs when large sections of the media share the same political views. Four large corporations own 88 percent of the British press. They also have interests in broadcasting. The result is that the media do not reflect the wide range of political views actually found in the country.

In many countries, journalists' associations and trade unions actively oppose open and secret censorship. Freedom of speech may be strengthened in some countries by government officials sometimes known as **ombudsmen**. It is the job of these officials to investigate complaints against the government, including that of unfair censorship.

POLITICS IN THE CLASSROOM

How can political censorship affect schoolchildren? In all schools, subjects for study are carefully selected. Subjects such as history, geography and social sciences are open to political influence.

In some countries, history books have been rewritten in order to fit in with the views of the government of the time. In the Soviet Union, in the year 1956, there was a major change of policy, regarding much of the country's recent past. The former leader, Joseph Stalin, who had died a few years earlier, was now toppled from his position as a national hero. As a result there was a brief period when all the schools were without history books – the old textbook which praised Stalin had been withdrawn, and the new version was still being prepared.

In some parts of the world, schoolchildren have had to learn history that is not their own. In colonial times, children in Africa and Asia learned instead about the faraway European countries which governed them. Once these newer nations became independent, they developed materials that gave their children the opportunity to learn about their own culture.

The language in which children are taught may also be a censorship issue in countries where there are several spoken languages. Many governments around the world only allow teaching to take place in one official language. Other languages may be banned.

Students demonstrating for greater political freedom in Tiananmen Square, May 1989. Army tanks were sent in by the government and many of the students were killed or jailed. All non-official posters and slogans, like the ones here, now have to be approved by the government.

Censorship can also be found in universities and centres for scientific research. In many countries, staff whose political views are unacceptable to the government may find that they do not receive grants to support them in their research. In some countries they may be fined, banned from foreign travel, or even imprisoned, or declared insane. A government can attempt to 'shut out' areas of knowledge or information that it feels are a threat. In South Korea for example, it is an offence to read or possess any literature from its communist neighbour, North Korea. Laws like this may be intended to protect the state, but they also prevent any genuine exchange of ideas amongst scholars and scientists.

RELIGIOUS FREEDOM?

**An angry demonstrator protests at a cinema showing
of *The Last Temptation of Christ*.**

Many religions are built upon the idea that they alone represent absolute truth. Judaism, Christianity and Islam all state clearly that there is only one God. **Atheists** believe that there is no God. **Agnostics** believe that the truth is unknown or cannot be fully understood by human beings. Religious censorship occurs in many situations – for example when there is conflict between different groups within the same faith, between faiths, or between believers and non-believers.

RELIGIOUS LAW

In some countries religious laws apply to all aspects of life. They are interpreted by priests. This is the case in Iran, which since 1979 has been governed according to Islamic *sharia* or law. Ancient Iranian literature and poetry was censored because it was not Islamic. Writings by people of the Bahai faith were banned. Documents in the state archives were destroyed. *Sharia* law was later introduced in Sudan and Pakistan.

In 1988 in Britain, a writer called Salman Rushdie published a novel called *The Satanic Verses*. Many Muslims around the world were offended by passages in the book. There were demonstrations against the author, and the book was publicly burned. In 1989 the Iranian leader, Ayatollah Khomeini, pronounced a *fatwa* against Salman Rushdie. This was a call to all Muslims to kill the author, out of duty to the Islamic faith. Many Muslims who did not like the book refused to accept such a call, but the author still had to go into hiding.

Muslims in England went to court in an attempt to have *The Satanic Verses* banned as blasphemous or offensive to the holy laws of Islam. They failed because the court ruled that the English law against blasphemy only applied to offences against the Christian faith. Many people felt that this was unfair, and that all religions should be protected in the same way. Others wished to see the offence of blasphemy abolished in Britain altogether, but attempts to change the law failed.

RELIGION AND STATE

In England (but not in Wales) there is an official or **established religion** which exists alongside government. The Queen is the head of the Church of England as well as the head of state. English law is not made by the Church, but it can be applied to religious beliefs. Blasphemy cases are still taken to court, and blasphemy must still be taken into account by the media. In 1989 the independent British Board of Film Classification (BBFC), which today controls film and video censorship, banned a video called *Visions of Esctasy* because it feared charges of blasphemy.

RELIGION AND EDUCATION

The United States constitution guarantees freedom of religious belief. There is no established religion.

> 'Congress shall make no law respecting an establishment of religion, or prohibiting the free exercise thereof...'
>
> *First Amendment, United States constitution*

However, religious censorship has occurred in some states as a result of pressure by citizens. In Alabama, large numbers of school books were banned because they put forward non-religious views. This decision was reversed by the federal courts, but the debate continues.

Another long-standing issue in some parts of the United States is the teaching of Darwin's theory of evolution. This scientific theory suggests that all life forms have developed gradually over millions of years. The belief is strongly disputed by **fundamentalist** Christians, who believe that every word of the Bible is literally true. The Bible states that the earth and all living things were created by God in six days. Teachers have sometimes been forbidden to teach Darwin's theory, and books have been banned.

ATHEIST STATES

Many communist states, including the Soviet Union and China, are officially atheist. They have censored all religious books and pamphlets and refused to allow religious services. Missionaries of all faiths have been prevented from spreading their ideas. Sometimes religious believers have been persecuted. At other times they have simply been discouraged. Sometimes priests required a government licence in order to preach. During periods of extreme censorship, believers from other countries sometimes attempted to smuggle religious books across borders. They faced severe punishment if caught.

Most atheist states now allow some form of religious worship to take place, even if they do not actively encourage it. Some still have strict laws. North Korea for example bans all publications which try to convert people to religious belief.

These Jews in Moscow are buying matzos for the Passover festival. At times the public sale of this special bread has been restricted by the Soviet authorities, as part of a general policy of discouraging religious practice.

MORAL AND DECENT?

American model Jerry Hall is followed by popular press reporters wherever she goes. Most famous people see this attention simply as a part of their life. If an ordinary person gets caught up in a news story, pressure from the media can ruin their privacy, and cause them great suffering.

What is moral and what is immoral? The answer often depends on people's religious, political or cultural views. These may also vary from one historical period to another. In the seventeenth century the Puritans thought that card-playing and going to the theatre were evil pastimes in themselves. Today, few people would take such an extreme view. Moral censorship in our own times is normally concerned with violence, bad language, sexual behaviour and racial equality. Other moral questions which enter the censorship debate include the honesty of advertisements and the fair treatment of individuals by the media.

> 'An editor is one who separates the wheat from the chaff and prints the chaff.'
>
> *Adlai Stevenson*
> *American politician (1900-65)*

A VIOLENT WORLD

Viewing figures released in the United States in 1988 claimed that, on average, an American child is likely to view about 26 000 murders on television before he or she is eighteen years old. We all know that television has a powerful influence on viewers. But does watching violence on screen make people behave violently? It is hard to prove. There have certainly been some terrible random murders where the killer is said to see himself as a figure like the violent film hero Rambo.

Some people say that violence on screen does not cause social problems, it simply reflects them. Certainly the television news each day includes scenes of warfare and violent crime. If such violence is censored, some people might argue that the truth is being hidden from the public.

In fact, censorship of screen violence takes place in most countries. There are many bodies such as the British Broadcasting Standards Council (BSC), founded in 1988 to vet programmes. Many countries license films and videos according to age limits. These are easy to enforce in a cinema, but harder in the home. Children may repeatedly see videos which are not suitable for their age group. It is often up to parents to act as censors in such a situation.

The problem is not limited to television, video and cinema. In 1951 and 1954, investigations by the United States Congress blamed comics for the increase in crime amongst young people. The publishers of comics had to set up a board which vetted and approved the content of their publications.

Language which gives offence to some people, such as swearing, has also been censored on television as well as on radio and in the theatre. Some complain that bad language too has a 'copycat effect', especially on young people. Many writers reply that they must be able to give a true picture of society and show people the way they are, even if this offends their audience.

DECENCY LAWS

In 1985 a United States Federal Commission was set up under Attorney General Edwin Meese. Its purpose was to look at new ways to control the 'problem of **pornography**'. In 1986 the Commission published a report demanding stricter law enforcement and harsh new censorship laws.

Pornography has existed for centuries. It has always been at the centre of the censorship debate. Many people believe that images of sex and nudity can, in the words of the British Obscene Publications Act, 'deprave and corrupt' the public. Some people object to pornography because it offends their religious or moral beliefs. Others believe that pornography degrades women, who are often shown more as sex objects than as people. They believe that pornography encourages violence towards women.

Others argue that there is not much evidence to prove that pornography corrupts. In countries that do not censor pornography harshly, such as the Netherlands, there do not appear to be more crimes of

Richard Nixon on the campaign trail for the United States presidency in 1968. Enormous sums of money are spent in America on promoting individual candidates, but normal advertising controls do not apply to political commercials. They are protected under the United States constitution. Critics of this system have said that political advertising is the most deceptive of all with regard to its promises to voters and its accusations against opponents.

violence against women, for example, than there is in countries where pornography is banned.

Sometimes governments or religious groups set out to control all kinds of matters which concern sex. Sex education may be banned in schools on the grounds that it encourages immorality amongst young people. Family planning advice may be banned in some Roman Catholic countries. Many teachers reject these controls. They claim instead that it is immoral to keep young people ignorant of sexual matters, when there is the risk of unwanted pregnancies or disease.

PROTECTING PEOPLE

Censorship may also be used to protect the rights of groups or individuals. Most journalists' professional codes, or rules, forbid them to write articles which encourage discrimination against different races or religions. In many countries it is now illegal to use the media to encourage racial hatred. However, people do still suffer from unfair treatment in the media. Sensational newspaper headlines often play on readers' own prejudices against particular groups – immigrants may be told to 'go home', peace movements may be ridiculed as 'soft', or labelled as 'subversive', homosexual groups or individuals may be described in insulting terms. Censorship laws can do little without a corresponding change in peoples' attitudes.

In an effort to change those attitudes, many schools and libraries ban story books which they feel encourage racism or **sexism**. Books which were written long ago may be included in such a ban, or even classic works that have been popular for generations. For example, books by Mark Twain have been banned in some American schools. Some people may ask why books that were written in a different age should be subjected to the standards we apply today. They think that such books can help us to understand the past, if they are published with a suitable explanation. Others believe that stories which reflect outdated views and prejudice are best forgotten.

FAIR PLAY

Some of the strongest pleas for control of the media come from individuals who believe that they are publicly wronged by an unfair book, newspaper article or broadcast. Most countries have laws of **libel**. It is a crime to publish words or pictures which attack someone's reputation. People can go to court to prevent the publication or broadcasting of such attacks. Threatening legal action is an effective method of censorship. Less common are laws of privacy, which protect individuals from being pestered by journalists, and laws which guarantee people the **right of reply** to accusations made against them through the media.

Advertising plays an increasingly important role in the media. It pays for most television broadcasting around the world. It can make up nearly 70 per cent of the income of a popular daily or Sunday newspaper. Many governments or watchdog bodies censor advertising. They ban advertisements which are misleading or dishonest. Some also restrict or ban advertising that is racist, sexist or offensive to various social groups. Advertisements that encourage unhealthy habits, such as drinking alcohol or smoking cigarettes, may also be banned or limited.

The World Federation of Advertisers believes that the advertising industry should censor its own commercials according to agreed guidelines, and this is indeed what happens in many countries. As companies become more international and television programmes cross national frontiers, there is an increasing need for internationally agreed advertising standards.

AROUND THE WORLD

The barbed wire candle is Amnesty International's symbol of remembrance for all prisoners of conscience. Here, it is being lit in a public ceremony in London by Michael Kyrkok. Michael's father – a member of the Greek parliament – was imprisoned by the military government that ruled Greece from 1967 to 1974.

FOR AND AGAINST

Today all of the world's 170 nations use censorship in some form or other, either all the time or under certain circumstances. There are human rights groups campaigning against censorship in most countries of the world. Some, such as the British Campaign for Press and Broadcasting Freedom, operate openly. In many countries, however, such groups are illegal and members may even risk jail or execution.

Writers may circulate illegally copied newspapers and books, sometimes known by the Russian term *samizdat*. In some countries, photocopiers and even typewriters must be licensed by the authorities. In recent years fax machines have been used to circulate illegal publications in the Soviet Union.

International human rights groups such as Amnesty International have successfully campaigned for the release of individuals who have been jailed for their beliefs. Groups such as Article 19 and PEN (the International Association of Poets, Playwrights, Editors, Essayists and Novelists) continue to campaign for freedom of speech.

There are also voluntary groups campaigning for more censorship. These may include anti-pornography and anti-violence campaigners such as the American Federation for Decency or, in Britain, Mary Whitehouse's Viewers' and Listeners' Association. They may include feminist or anti-racist groups which are campaigning for more control over the media treatment of women or ethnic groups.

The censorship debate is not one which has any neat solutions. Most of us approve of a free press, but few of us can agree as to what that means. Most of us approve of free speech, but can think of situations where that freedom might serve the cause of injustice – should one be free to lie or to stir up hatred, for example?

INTERNATIONAL AGREEMENTS

Even if censorship issues can never be solved once and for all, it is vitally important that they remain at the centre of international treaties and conferences. In 1948 the United Nations Organization passed a Universal Declaration of Human Rights. It included a section regarding censorship:

'Everyone has the right to freedom of opinion and expression; this right includes freedom to hold opinions without interference and to seek, receive and impart information and ideas through any media and regardless of frontiers.'

This statement was not observed by member states at the time and is still not observed today. It does however remain a worthwhile aim for the future. It has influenced the drawing up of agreements around the world, such as the African Charter on Human and Peoples' Rights and the American Convention on Human Rights, which is signed by 19 countries (but not the United States or Canada).

The Council of Europe established a European Convention on Human Rights in 1950. Complaints by states or by individuals, many involving questions of censorship, are looked into by a commission. If a legal case can be made, this may be forwarded to the Committee of Ministers or to the European Court of Human Rights in Strasbourg, founded in 1959. Britain had more findings against it in the period up to 1987 than any other member nation.

Human rights, including freedom of speech, have today entered into most international agreements. They usually follow a long way behind economic and political interests. However, the fact that censorship is still an issue today offers hope for the future.

'The task is to find a legal framework that will protect freedom of expression while dealing with the abuse of human sensibility, whether sexual, social, or political.'

Nadine Gordimer,
South African writer, 1990

KEY DATES

BC 443
First public censor Powerful Roman officials to organize population counts, supervise public behaviour and judge whether literature is suitable.

BC 213
Burning the books Chinese emperor Qin Shi Huangdi orders destruction of all literature that is not strictly practical.

AD 1559
The Church as censor Congregation of the Index set up to vet all books published in Roman Catholic countries.

1791
Freedom in the New World... A Bill of Rights is included in the new American constitution which guarantees free speech to all citizens.

1792
...but fear of revolution in Britain Thomas Paine publishes his enormously successful *Rights of Man* in England, but has to flee to France to escape trial for treason.

1818
Protecting the public? Thomas Bowdler publishes *The Family Shakespeare*, a censored edition of Shakespeare's plays considered suitable for family reading.

1943
Cultural blackout Theatres and most publishing houses in Germany closed by Nazi propaganda minister during the Second World War. Elsewhere news is reported under wartime restrictions.

1950-4
Fear of the bogeyman Senator Joseph McCarthy attacks suspected 'communists' in the United States and accuses them of 'un-American activities' in front of TV cameras.

1961
Working for free speech Foundation of Amnesty International, a campaigning organization dedicated to help victims of censorship and of other human rights abuse world wide.

1986
Challenging official secrets In the *Spycatcher* court case, the British government fails to get former secret service agent Peter Wright's book suppressed.

1989
Islam and the laws of blasphemy Muslim leader of Iran, Ayatollah Khomeini, pronounces a death sentence on Salman Rushdie, author of *The Satanic Verses*. Many Muslims regard the book as blasphemous, but the British blasphemy laws only applied to Christianity.

GLOSSARY

agnostic Someone who is not sure whether God exists.

atheist Someone who believes that there is no god at all.

authoritarian A style of government that tells people what to do, and does not allow them to join in the decision making.

blasphemous Offending the holy laws of a religious faith.

censorship Preventing free communication of ideas between people.

classified Information that might be a risk to national security.

democratic Any form of government in which rule is by the people or by their elected representatives. Many states in the world call themselves democratic but in reality very few are.

dissident Disagreeing with public opinion or government policy. A person who disagrees in this way is known as a dissident.

established religion Official, or authorized by the state.

expurgate To make a book `pure' by removing any parts of it that people might think are improper.

fundamentalist Someone who believes that everything written in the scriptures of a religion is the literal truth.

heretic Somebody who rejects accepted religious views or holds different beliefs.

immoral Judged to be wrong by society or by an individual.

jamming Blocking a radio message with noise interference.

libel To unfairly damage someone's good name in print or in pictures. Libel is a criminal offence.

media Organizations used for communications, such as the press, radio and television.

obscene Something that is indecent, or highly offensive. Most countries have laws which can be used against, for example, obscene publications or displays.

official secret Government information which by law may not be made known to the public.

ombudsman Someone who is appointed by a government to report on complaints from the people about government methods or public services.

pornography Images or words intended to excite sexual desire.

prudish Over-modest, easily shocked, or narrow-minded.

racist Emphasizing differences or encouraging hatred between races or ethnic groups.

right of reply The right of a person or group wronged by the media to have their reply published in return.

sexism The belief that one sex is superior to another, or that one form of sexual behaviour is better than another.

suppress To prevent publication of printed material. Political opinions may also be suppressed, for example, by the banning of public meetings.

treasonable Proposing the overthrow of a ruler or the betrayal of a country.

vetting The process of checking a person or an object against a set of rules.

whistle-blower Somebody who breaks their work contract in the public interest, by revealing secret activities. They may work for a firm or a department of government.

INDEX